THE UNDOING OF CONSERVATISM

John Gray

The Social Market Foundation
1994

First published in June 1994
by
The Social Market Foundation
20, Queen Anne's Gate
London SW1H 9AA
Tel: 071-222 7060 Fax: 071-222 0310

Paper No. 21

ISBN 1 874097 45 3

Cover design by Adrian Taylor

Printed in Great Britain by
Xenogamy plc
Suite 2, Westcombe House
7-9 Stafford Road, Wallington, Surrey SM6 9AN
Typesetting by Wimyk Enterprises

CONTENTS

THE AUTHOR

JOHN GRAY is a Fellow of Jesus College, Oxford and a member of the board of the Social Market Foundation. He is the author of *Mill on liberty: a defence, Hayek on liberty, Liberalism, Post-liberalism* and *Beyond the New Right*.

ACKNOWLEDGEMENTS

In this paper a train of thought developed in my book, *Beyond the New Right*, is brought to a conclusion. In that book, I attacked the New Right for its fundamentalist conception of market institutions and its hubristic ideological neglect of the human need for common life. My argument in that book ended with a defense of traditional conservatism, qualified by concerns about environmental integrity and stability suggested by Green thought. My argument in this paper is that the hegemony within conservative thought of Neo-Liberal ideology is so complete that there is now no historical or political possibility of a return to traditional conservatism. Further, the novelty of the dilemmas we face renders any attempt at a recovery of traditional conservatism profitless and anachronistic. Neo-Liberalism has only finished off a process which the nature and needs of our age had already taken a long way — the dissolution of any recognisable Tory philosophy. This paper may be read as a provisional first step toward thinking afresh at a time when conservative thought — along with the other traditions of political reflection, liberal and socialist — has become powerless to guide us.

I wish to thank Danny Finkelstein for his helpful comments on the first draft of this paper and Alastair Kilmarnock for his kindness in showing me his writings on economic growth. Comments by Fred Ikle have enabled me to clarify my argument at several points.

Conversations with Sir James Goldsmith have been important in stirring my thoughts on many of the questions discussed in this paper. Conversations with Edward Goldsmith have helped me understand the relations of economic and ecological systems in several ways, particularly the importance (from the standpoint of social stability) of limiting the disembedding of market institutions from local economies.

Responsibility for this paper remains mine alone.

Foreword

The Undoing of Conservatism is the result of more than a decade's thought by its author. During this period John Gray has become one of the most important contemporary critics of rationalism in politics. In the early 1980s he began to argue that the well-spring of Hayek's work is a conception of human knowledge and the mind as 'a domain of mystery governed by rules whose content we cannot discover'. By the end of the decade he had developed a fuller critique drawing on the work of Michael Polanyi of what he called the 'epistemic impossibilities of successful central planning'. In his more recent work he has expanded this criticism of rationalism to the work of Neo-Liberals, arguing in his book *Beyond the New Right* that 'it is not a plan to end all planning that will protect us from collectivism; as Oakshott says pointedly of Hayek, such a plan is of the same style of politics as that which it seeks to resist'. He has added to this assault on universalism writing in his Social Market Foundation Paper *Post-Communist Societies in Transition* of the mistaken idea 'that there is a single ideal-typical form of market institution to which all economies will, or should, approximate', and positing instead 'the primacy of cultural tradition in political life'.

In this powerful Paper Gray draws together these themes and uses them to argue that there is a crisis in Conservatism. He argues that economic imperialism and libertarianism have triumphed over the caution and traditionalism of Conservative thought. The result has been that the institutions that underpin the social order and entrench market activities in civic culture are being swept away by the philosophy of progress and the economics of unfettered markets. Conservatives, he believes, may attempt a retreat to cultural fundamentalism to escape the consequences of the 'progress' they have encouraged but the result will inevitably be failure — we have 'progressed' too far for retreat to be an option.

John Gray's Paper shares with David Willetts' *Civic Conservatism* a belief that free markets are legal institutions dependent on social consent rather than abstract and universal theory. However the authors part company when considering the possibilities and consequences of growth, with Gray sharply pessimistic.

Whether or not one shares Gray's pessimism and his call, for instance, for GATT to be abandoned, his analysis of the moral and historical foundations of market institutions, of which this Paper is just a part, is a vital element in a reassessment of free market thought and how its insights and benefits contribute to liberty and free association.

Daniel Finkelstein
June 1994

Introduction: Conservatism In Retrospect

The undoing of conservatism has come about as an unintended consequence of Hayekian policy. The hegemony, within conservative thought and practice, of Neo-Liberal ideology has had the effect of destroying conservatism as a viable political project in our time. Traditional conservatism is no longer a realistic political option when inherited institutions and practices have been swept away by the market forces which Neo-Liberal policies release or reinforce. When our institutional inheritance — that precious and irreplaceable patrimony of mediating structures and autonomous professions — is thrown away in the pursuit of a managerialist Cultural Revolution seeking to remodel the entire national life on the impoverished model of contract and market exchange, it is clear that the task of conserving and renewing a culture is no longer understood by contemporary conservatives. In the context of such a Maoism of the Right, it is the permanent revolution of unfettered market processes, not the conservation of traditional institutions and professions, having each of them a distinctive *ethos*, that has become the ruling project of contemporary conservatism. At the same time, Neo-Liberalism itself can now be seen as a self-undermining political project. Its political success depended upon cultural traditions, and constellations of interests that Neo-Liberal policy was bound to dissipate. In adopting the Neo-Liberal programme of a permanent institutional revolution as their own, contemporary conservatives have not only abandoned any claim to be guardians of continuity in national life; they have at the same time linked their fortunes to a political project which all the evidence suggests is self-defeating.

In the late Seventies, and throughout the earlier years of the Eighties, Neo-Liberalism was a compelling response to otherwise intractable dilemmas. The manifest failings of corporatist policy in Britain and the collapse of central planning throughout the Soviet bloc vindicated market institutions as the chief organising structures in any modern economy. The old 'systems debate', between 'planning' and 'markets', was resolved decisively on the terrain of history. By the late Eighties, however, that old debate receded, and a new debate began to emerge —

a debate about the varieties and limits of market institutions, and about their cultural and political preconditions. In this new debate, Neo-Liberal thought has little to contribute. Further, conservative policy that is animated by Neo-Liberal ideology finds itself baffled and powerless when confronted by the political challenges to market institutions that distinguish the Nineties — well exemplified in the success of neo-communist parties as the principal political beneficiaries of market reform in the post-Soviet world. In Western democracies, such as Britain, Canada and New Zealand, conservative governments animated by free market ideology look, impotent and aghast, into an electoral abyss which their own policies have opened up for them. Yet the option of returning to an older conservatism — 'One Nation' Toryism in Britain, say — has been closed for them by the social effects of market forces whose often destructive radicalism conservative policies have only enhanced. As a result, conservatism, in Britain and elsewhere, has arrived at an intellectual and political impasse, from which it can neither advance nor retreat. Except in societies, such as Italy, whose special histories have given it a further lease on life, conservatism is now a spent force in most Western countries. In an irony that will delight historians in years to come, the political effect of the ephemeral intellectual hegemony of the New Right, in Britain and similar countries, has probably been to accomplish the political destruction of conservatism: it may have rendered conservative parties unelectable, perhaps for a generation.

The capture of conservative parties and governments throughout the Western world by free market ideology was an accomplished and familiar fact by the late Eighties. Its full implications have yet to be properly understood. The conquest of modern Western conservatism by a species of market fundamentalism — Manchesterism *redivivus* — has transformed it profoundly and probably irreversibly. A political outlook that in Burke, Disraeli and Salisbury was sceptical of the project of the Enlightenment and suspicious of the promise of progress has mortgaged its future on a wager on indefinite economic growth and unfettered market forces. Such a bet — Hayek's wager, as it might be called — scarcely exhibits the political prudence which was once revered as a conservative virtue. It leaves the governments and societies that have staked their patrimony on such a throw defenceless and without resources when, in the normal fortunes of markets everywhere, or because economic growth has come up against insuperable social or ecological limits, market institutions fail to deliver the goods expected of them. In such circumstances, liberal civilisation itself may be imperiled, insofar as its legitimacy has been linked with the utopia of perpetual growth powered by unregulated market processes, and the inevitable failure of this utopia spawns illiberal political movements.

Indeed, unconstrained market institutions are bound to undermine social and political stability, particularly as they impose on the population unprecedented levels of economic insecurity with all the resultant dislocations of life in families and communities. Market-driven economic change, especially when it is large-scale, rapid and unremitting, fosters insecurity also by marginalising traditional forms and confounding established expectations. In the countries of continental Europe, the emergence of high levels of structural unemployment has been accompanied by the re-emergence of atavistic parties of the Right. In Britain, the desolation of communities by unchannelled market forces and the resultant pervasive sense of economic insecurity have not, and in all likelihood will not, evoke similar illiberal political movements; but they have been crucial factors in an epidemic of crime that probably has no parallel in national life since the early nineteenth century. It is only by the exercise of heroic powers of self-deception, or else by simple dishonesty, that British Conservatives can fail to discern the links between levels of criminality that are unprecedented in recent generations and policies of marketisation, pursued for a decade and a half, which have ridden roughshod over settled communities and established expectations. It is only a similar exercise in self-delusion or economy with the truth that can blind Conservatives to the links between the economic changes which their policies have reinforced and accelerated and the growth of the many varieties of poverty which are indifferently lumped together under the fashionable but deeply misconceived category of the underclass.

It is a general truth that, when they are disembedded from any context of common life, and emancipated from political constraints, market forces — especially when they are global — work to unsettle communities and delegitimate traditional institutions. This is a truism, no doubt; but it expresses an insight — that, for most people, security against risk is more important than the enhancement of choice — that conservative parties and governments have forgotten. For many people, perhaps most, the largely illusory enhancement of choice through freeing up markets does not compensate for the substantial increase in insecurity it also generates. More specifically, Neo-Liberal policies have worked to extend to the middle classes the insecurities and risks that have always plagued working-class life. By framing their policies with reference to an Enlightenment ideology of world-betterment through unconstrained global markets, Western conservatives may have given the *rentier* a new lease on life; but they have also brought about the euthanasia of the old middle classes . The political price to be paid for this dubious achievement is likely to be high, and, in the British case, may conceivably be the destruction of the Conservative Party — in its present form at any rate — as a party of government.

In throwing in its lot with the cult of the free market Western conservatism has colluded with the spirit of the age, which is well summarised in Hayek's candidly nihilistic dictum 'Progress is movement for movement's sake'.[1] Conservatives who imagine that their parties can be recovered for traditional values are deluding themselves. New political groupings may arise, in which genuinely conservative ideas coexist with, and are fertilised by, ideas from other traditions; but the notion that established conservative parties can be reclaimed, and turned into vehicles for an older conservative philosophy is, in most countries, a mere illusion. The result of conservative policy over the past decade and a half has been to junk traditional practices of all sorts in the pursuit of the mirage of the wholly free market; the evident fact that the workings of unconstrained market institutions might be incompatible with the stability of any real-world society is treated as a taboo in conservative political discourse. Equally, the possibility — indeed, the reality — that policies predicated on the prospect of open-ended economic growth neglect the fragility of the natural world of which our species is but a part has been thoroughly exorcised from consciousness. In attaching themselves to the utopia of perpetual growth in goods and services , conservatives have surrendered abjectly to the spirit of the age. To attempt to return conservative parties, or for that matter Western societies, to traditional forms of life at this stage in our history is to tilt at windmills, or else to enter into a dangerous flirtation with forms of cultural fundamentalism whose upshot will be — like the ephemeral 'Back to Basics' campaign of the Major Government

— at best farcical. The better way lies in the recognition that in our circumstances renewing genuine conservative values, and passing on the traditions of a liberal civilisation, demand novel and radical policies and a willingness to think in unorthodox ways. Recent conservative thought is of no more assistance in this task than traditional socialist thought.

A central test of the readiness to think fresh thoughts is the way we think about market institutions. On the view defended here they are not ends in themselves but means or tools whose end is human well-being. Those who apply a model of the free market that was useful in the struggle against the stagnant corporatism of the Seventies to the radically different problems of the Nineties are misapplying liberal ideas in a fashion that is dangerous to liberal civilisation itself. If the threat to a liberal form of life came in the Seventies from an invasive and overly ambitious state, in the Nineties it comes from the desolation and collapse of communities and the excesses of individualism, which have in fact been compounded by policies which conceive of marketisation as an all-purpose cure-all for economic and social ills. If, in the Seventies, the principal danger to liberal civilisation came from the hubris of government, in the Eighties and Nineties it has come from hubristic liberal ideology, in which a fetish is made of individual choice and the needs of solidarity and common life go unrecognised or spurned. The starting point for serious political discourse in Britain in the Nineties must be in the recognition that the paleo-liberal celebration of consumer choice and market freedom as the only undisputed values has become a recipe for *anomie*, social breakdown and ultimately economic failure.

This is not to say that there are not areas of policy in which market institutions can still be usefully extended: there is a good case, as I shall suggest in Chapter Seven of this paper, for the introduction of a version of the educational voucher that is different in crucial respects from those proposed by Neo-Liberals, with the aim of anchoring schooling more deeply in local communities. And, always provided such measures are fully and properly funded, there may be a useful role for analogous voucher schemes in some areas of welfare policy. Equally, not all curbs on market freedoms that are presently in place, or currently envisaged, are sensible, or defensible in any terms that are recognisably liberal: there is much in recent EU proposals — for the restriction of vitamins as forms of prescription medicine and for the restraint of commercial expression, for example — that smacks of the moralism and paternalism that would immediately, and rightly, be rejected by liberal opinion in other areas of policy.[2] From the truth that market freedom is not a dogma it does not follow that current or proposed restraints on market freedoms are always acceptable. The deeper truth is that market institutions are useful devices, not articles of faith. Their scope, varieties and limits cannot be known *a priori*, but are to be assessed tentatively and provisionally. Such assessment will turn on the contribution they make to human well-being and their impact on valuable cultural traditions and forms of common life. Importantly, since cultural forms are various, the proper scope and limits of market freedoms will also be variable. Abstract notions of choice or rights are of very little use in sensible reflection on markets and their limits. Consumer choice, for example, is an important good, still sometimes wrongly curtailed, whose justification is in its contribution to individual empowerment. It cannot nevertheless be the basis of an entire political philosophy, or of the whole agenda of public policy.

When applied, or misapplied, in the context of a Neo-Liberal ideology that is insensitive to the human needs for community and cultural identity, the idea of consumer choice becomes positively pernicious. To make a fetish of free trade, for example, when it manifestly does not serve human needs, risks discrediting market institutions, and endangers the stability of liberal societies. Yet this risk will become a reality, wherever market institutions are presented not as indispensable instruments for the achievement of individual and communal objectives, to be shaped and curbed by reference to those ends, but as an all-or-nothing package, which has only an incidental (or coincidental) connexion with the communities and cultures it serves. The real danger of paleo-liberal thought and policy in all of its forms is that it does not understand that market institutions are stable and enduring only insofar as they are embedded in the common cultures of those whose needs they exist to serve.

This is a danger that is being incurred not only by free market conservatism but also by traditional varieties of the Left project, all of which stake their policies on a resumption of economic growth — on a species of revived Croslandism. Insofar as the Left project remains wedded to growthmanship, and fails to respond to the challenge of a situation in which a resumption of economic growth on conventional lines is unachievable or undesirable, it will suffer the same fate of political obsolescence that has befallen the market liberal doctrines of the New Right. Nor have recent attempts to reformulate a New Left project confronted the obstacles to socialist ideals presented by conventional prescriptions for global free trade.[3] At present, all conventional political thought seems fixated on assumptions, such as the possibility and desirability of resuming economic growth at the rates and of the sorts experienced in the Eighties or the Sixties, and on models, such as those of Anglo-American individualist capitalism or European social democracy, which have clearly had their day. There is a real danger that the ossification of liberal thought resulting from the hegemony of discredited Neo-Liberal ideas in all mainstream parties opens a window of political opportunity for avowed enemies of liberal civilisation. The gap between received political ideas and present political realities has rarely been wider, or more perilous. We will best conserve our liberal patrimony if, as Maynard Keynes urged us to do, we seek new wisdom for a new age. The beginning of such wisdom is in the recognition that Western conservatism has come undone in its adoption of the policies and philosophy of the unfettered free market.

The Strange Death Of Free Market Conservatism

What must be true for conservatism to be possible? This question is likely be received as a donnish diversion from serious political thought. Its implication — that, whatever the preconditions of conservatism may be, they may no longer exist among us today — may seem especially frivolous. For virtually all Western countries have political parties that avow themselves to be conservative; there are, or have been lately, groups which meet to consider the principles of conservative philosophy; and it has been cogently argued by one of our most modern and least nostalgist writers that a conservative disposition remains an essential element in any life that is recognisable by us, in whom the passion for novelty and the penchant for choice-making are notably strong, as worth living.[4] Given these familiar considerations, an inquiry into the presuppositions of conservatism may well appear to be ill-considered. And certain well-known features of conservative thought would seem to make an exploration of its general preconditions an especially unpromising venture. After all, what could be more misconceived than an effort at a transcendental deduction of a political outlook that disdains abstract principle, favours the local over the universal, and denies that practice needs support from philosophical 'foundations'? The search for the necessary preconditions of conservatism may even be dismissed as arising from a misunderstanding of conservatism itself.

Yet it will be my contention that the question with which I have begun is far from frivolous. I will argue instead that the conditions under which conservatism as a coherent form of political thought and practice are possible exist no longer; that conservatism has for us a Cheshire cat quality, in that what it proposes to conserve is a spectral thing, voided of substance, partly by the policies of recent conservative governments and partly by aspects of modern societies which such policies have reinforced; and that conservative parties and movements have in all Western countries been captured by Neo-Liberal ideas, more properly thought of as those of fundamentalist or classical liberalism, which in their utopian projects of world-improvement and their expectation of convergence on a universal civilisation are alien to the forms of thought and practice most characteristic of a conservative outlook as that used to be understood.

At the same time, I will submit that any political outlook that is merely reactionary in its response to the dilemmas of the late modern period in which we live is bound to be a form of quixotry, or else of atavism. Ironically, and ominously, it is the capture of conservative parties by a primitive species of paleo-liberalism — which is what Neo-Liberalism and Neo-Conservatism really are — that enhances the prospects of truly atavistic illiberal movements. In a mirror irony, the hegemony within conservative thought and practice of market liberalism, when combined with the disruptive effects of unfettered market forces on settled communities and inherited social forms, has the result that unreflective adherence to tradition has been destroyed and replaced, if at all, by varieties of religious or cultural fundamentalism. In short, the subversive effects of unhampered market institutions on traditional forms of life makes free-market conservatism an inherently unstable and, over time, a self-undermining political project. For these reasons, I conclude that a genuinely conservative form of political thought and practice, the lineaments of which we can discern as at least one element in our cultural history, is no longer a real possibility for us. How has this strange circumstance come about?

The Self-Destruction Of Traditional Conservatism

The conquest in the Eighties of conservative parties throughout the world by doctrines of market liberalism did not come out of the blue. At least since the end of the Second World War conservative parties in Western countries had relied upon policies which stimulated economic growth as the principal means of securing the political legitimacy of market institutions. In conditions of rapid economic growth the destructive impact of market forces on communities and settled practices is softened, or compensated by, the new opportunities that such growth affords. Further, the dislocations occasioned by market competition can in such conditions be palliated by welfare institutions and more fundamental issues of distribution and livelihood taken off the political agenda. This was, in effect, the Butskellite settlement in postwar British political life: social conflict was avoided by the pursuit of a full employment policy and by the establishment of a welfare state in which the middle classes participated fully, which were funded by the proceeds of economic growth. Post-war British governments until 1979 conceived their task as that of extending their hold on office by aligning the electoral and the political cycles in a context of sustained economic growth. Whether or not particular governments were successful in this feat, the adoption of this conception of their task by the two major parties in Britain produced a period of political and social stability in Britain that began to unravel only in the late Seventies. Moreover, the postwar settlement in Britain was paralleled by similar settlements in all the major Western countries, and began to show signs of strain in many of them in the late Seventies and early Eighties.

The chief innovation of early Thatcherism in Britain was to tear up the post-war social compact — at least as that concerned macro-economic policies aiming at full employment and at a smooth meshing of the economic and political cycles — by the adoption of the Medium Term Financial Strategy (MTFS). The welfare state was left comparatively intact, but the political thrust of early Thatcherism was in the direction of the dismantlement of the corporatist policies of the Sixties and early Seventies, by the dissolution of the triangular relationship between government, business and the trade unions on which corporatist policy was based. It is important to note that these corporatist relationships started to come unstuck in Britain well before the coming to power of Margaret Thatcher in 1979. The Healey-IMF squeeze of the last Labour government was a clear portent of the fiscal austerity pursued in the early Thatcher years. It is no less important to be clear that when the collusive corporatism of the Sixties and Seventies foundered it was because it had issued in stagflation and social conflict, rather than yielding steady economic growth and social peace. Corporatism had failed to deliver the goods; but the idea that market institutions can secure political legitimacy in a democratic regime only against a background of steady growth in output remained firmly in place. The central project of early Thatcherism, whose intellectual inspiration came from rational expectations theory in economics, from the utopian notion of an economic constitution proposed in the Public Choice school and from the *melange* of classical liberal and libertarian ideas that came together briefly under the heading of the New Right, was to secure the conditions of economic growth by the setting up of a stable framework of rules rather than by government acting directly as a pacemaker of economic expansion.

Though, predictably, the MTFS came to grief in the mid-Eighties, the rewriting of the British social compact that it embodied had political resonance into the early Nineties. It is arguable that the result of the 1992 General Election can be better explained by the decoupling in voters' perceptions of the performance of government from that of the economy than by mistrust of Labour's economic competence. This decoupling, in turn, was probably the most enduring trace of over a decade of Thatcherite rhetoric and statecraft focusing on the autonomy of market forces — a tribute to the success of Thatcherism, for a while at least, as a hegemonic political project whose objective was the transformation of British political culture. Whether this alteration in voters' perceptions is in fact irreversible or even long-lasting is another matter, but fortunately not one which anything fundamental in the present argument turns on. For, even if the correlation between voting behaviour and perceived economic well-being has been irreversibly weakened in British political life, the electoral prospects of British conservatism are not thereby necessarily enhanced. An upswing in the economy will not then work inevitably in favour of a sitting Conservative Government, and elections will turn on other issues. Most likely, the traces of this Thatcherite legacy, in conjunction with the stubborn reality of persistently slow growth, will alter the terms of political trade by shifting the content of public discourse in Britain. The parties will be assessed by the voters on how they address issues having to do with the quality of life rather than on narrow issues of economic management. Specifically, they will be judged on how they propose to protect the quality of life in Britain more than upon their policies for the rekindling of economic growth. In other words, low growth — an annual growth rate of around two percent or so, say — seems likely to be a presupposition of political debate in Britain, as perhaps in other European countries, for the foreseeable future. This is a prospect that bodes ill for the political fortunes of conservatism insofar as it continues to be wedded to the growth-oriented doctrines of market liberalism.

The deepest difficulty of contemporary conservatism is that of securing the political legitimacy of the unfettered market institutions to which it is committed in an age of low economic growth. In such an age, the gale of creative destruction blows less benignly, with the processes of entrepreneurship and technological innovation which distinguish unencumbered market institutions eliminating jobs without generating new ones of the same sort or at the same rate. The dystopian prospect — not so far, perhaps, from the present reality — is of a highly dynamic but low-growth economy in which a permanent revolution in technologies and productive arrangements yields large-scale structural unemployment and pervasive job insecurity. As Edward Luttwak has noted, in his provocative piece on 'Why Fascism is the Wave of the Future': 'Structural change, with all its personal upheavals and social disruptions, is now quite rapid even when there is zero growth, becoming that much faster when economies do grow. The engine turns, grinding lives and grinding down established human relationships, even when the car is stopped; and reaches Ferrari-like rpms at the most modest steamroller speeds.' Luttwak comments: ' ... neither the moderate Right nor the moderate Left even recognises, let alone offers any solution for, the central problem of our days: the completely unprecedented personal economic insecurity of working people, from industrial workers and white-collar clerks to medium-high managers.'[5]

The fact that the subversive dynamism of market institutions, particularly when these are globalised, destroys personal and communal economic security even in conditions of zero economic growth is of central importance not only in the Western liberal democracies of which Luttwak is speaking primarily, but also for the post-communist states. For, in the latter, the collapse of bankrupt institutions of central planning, and the subsequent ill-conceived adoption of Neo-Liberal policies of shock-therapy, has replicated in grotesquely exaggerated form the Western problem of market-driven structural economic adjustments occurring in conditions of zero or even negative growth. Entirely predictably, though evoking the baffled incomprehension of Western opinion, the political beneficiaries of mass economic insecurity pervasive in such conditions have, virtually everywhere, been neo-communist parties and neo-fascist parties, sometimes in combination. In many, indeed most of the post-communist states, the political risk of unregulated market institutions that are exposed to the full gale of global market forces — namely that the liberal institutions that are supposed (according to Western theory) to accompany them will be repudiated or compromised — has already generated a powerful backlash against Western-imposed policies of shock therapy. It is paradoxical, but typical of the intellectual confusion of the times, that politicians and parties in the post-communist countries that seek to temper the impact of market reform on an already shell-shocked society, and thereby to preserve a measure of social and political stability, are denounced by Western conservatives for their deviations from Neo-Liberal orthodoxy. These developments in the post-communist countries have so far been little noted or comprehended in the West. They contain lessons that Western political elites and opinion formers show few signs of learning. The fundamental truth that rapid and continuous market-driven economic change is inimical to settled community, and in the longer run to the stability of liberal and democratic institutions, has apparently yet to be grasped by most Western policy-makers.

The fact that the mobility of labour required of everyone in a society dominated by unconstrained market institutions is profoundly disruptive of settled communities and imposes severe strains on life in families is neglected, or repressed, by those contemporary conservatives — the vast majority — for whom the United States is the tacit or explicit model. It is true enough that, in the American case, all other values have been sacrificed for the sake of micro-economic flexibility, productivity and low labour costs. This American model, which is unlikely to be replicated as successfully anywhere else, has to its credit that the relentless pursuit of efficiency has kindled renewed economic growth, spurred technological advance and generated millions of new jobs. At the same time, the American model of individualist market institutions has been distinguished by levels of family breakdown and fractured community, of criminality and of incarceration, that are unknown in other Western countries. In addition, the successes in job creation in America have necessitated a large-scale casualisation of work, a lowering of real incomes in the middle classes and a revolution of falling expectations in the younger generation that will not be tolerated in any European country.

The American model, in which economic growth is restarted, against all the odds in a mature industrial economy, by restructuring and technological innovation in an atomised labour market, is not exportable to any society with a less individualist moral and political culture. Yet it is the paradigm for policy in all conservative parties in which market liberalism is dominant. Contrary to the American neo-conservative view which market liberals in other countries have endorsed, America is not in any sense a model for a universal civilisation, but rather a singularity, a limiting case, whose lessons for others are chiefly negative. The significance of the American example for older and more rooted cultures is, in fact, of a warning to be heeded rather than of a model to be emulated. For the adoption in these older cultures of an American model for economic policy is bound to entail far greater cultural losses, with most of the economic gains being small, speculative or entirely illusory. If there can be such a thing as a coherent form of conservative thought and policy in the European countries — and it is an implication of my argument that that is at best an open question — then it can only be one that has decoupled, economically, politically and culturally, from the American exemplar which animates the New Right.

Market liberalism, as we have come to know it in Britain and elsewhere in the Eighties, fosters a privileging of choice and a cult of mobility that consort badly with the settled communities cherished by traditional conservatives. Indeed, among us, market liberalism is in its workings ineluctably subversive of tradition and community. This may not have been the case in Edmund Burke's day, in which the maintenance of the traditions of Whig England could coexist with a policy of economic individualism, but in our age a belief in any such harmony is a snare and a delusion. Among us, unlike the men and women of Burke's day, markets are global, and also, in the case of capital markets, nearly instantaneous; free trade, if it too is global, operates among communities that are vastly more uneven in development than any that traded with one another in Burke's time; and our lives are pervaded by mass media that transform tastes, and revolutionise daily habits, in ways that could be only dimly glimpsed by the Scottish political economists whom Burke so revered.

For the Scottish thinkers to whom Burke owed allegiance, there was nevertheless no pre-ordained harmony between the workings of a commercial society and the renewal of valued traditions. Adam Smith feared that the minute division of labour required in the emerging commercial society would stultify popular sensibility and intellectual development, and worried that the anonymity of great towns would lead to a breakdown in informal social monitoring; he conjectured that the dissociation of market success from the moral virtues in commercial societies could generate a new and perverse form of emulation, and that the hedonism of commercial societies would make the martial virtues unsustainable in them. As Smith himself put it, in one of his lectures on jurisprudence: 'There are some inconveniences ... arising from a commercial spirit. The first we shall mention is that it confines the views of men. Where the division of labour is brought to perfection, every man has only a simple operation to perform. To this his whole attention is confined, and few ideas pass in his mind but what have an immediate connexion with it ... Another inconvenience attending commerce is that education is greatly neglected ... we find that in the commercial parts of England, the tradesmen are for the most part in this despicable condition: their work through half the week is sufficient to maintain them, and thro' want of education they have no amusement for the other but riot and debauchery. So it may very justly be said that the people who cloath the whole world are in rags themselves ... Another bad effect of commerce is that it sinks the courage of mankind and tends to extinguish the martial spirit. In all commercial countries the division of labour is infinite, and every ones thoughts are employed on one particular thing ... In the same manner war comes to be a trade also ... The defence of the country is therefore committed to a certain set of men who have nothing else to do; and among the bulk of the people military courage diminishes.'[6]

These concerns, shared by other Scottish thinkers such as Adam Ferguson, have scarcely been shown to be groundless or exaggerated by the subsequent history of market societies. Most of Smith's latter-day epigones seem nevertheless not to have taken to heart his wise summary and conclusion:' These are the disadvantages of a commercial spirit. The minds of men are contracted and rendered incapable of elevation, education is despised or at least neglected, and heroic spirit is almost utterly extinguished. To remedy these defects would be an object worthy of serious attention.'[7] These moral and cultural shortcomings of a commercial society, so vividly captured by one of its seminal theorists, figure less prominently, if at all, in the banal discourse of free market ideology.

The social and cultural effects of market liberalism are, virtually without exception, inimical to the values that traditional conservatives hold dear. Communities are scattered to the winds by the gale of creative destruction. Endless 'downsizing' and 'flattening' of enterprises fosters ubiquitous insecurity and makes loyalty to the company a cruel joke. The celebration of consumer choice, as the only undisputed value in market societies, devalues commitment and stability in personal relationships and encourages the view of marriage and the family as vehicles of self-realisation. The dynamism of market processes dissolves social hierarchies and overturns established expectations. Status is ephemeral, trust frail and contract sovereign. The dissolution of communities promoted by market-driven labour mobility weakens, where it does not entirely destroy, the informal social monitoring of behaviour which is the most effective preventive measure against crime. It is odd that British conservatives, who have followed their American teachers in blaming the rise in crime in Britain on the disincentive effects of welfare measures, have not noticed that most forms of crime (apart from some sorts of property crime) are vastly commoner in the United States, where welfare institutions are far less developed, and market-driven labour mobility and its resultant *anomie* far more intense.

It is a general truth that has gone little noted by contemporary conservatives that the incessant change promoted and demanded by market processes nullifies the significance of precedent and destroys the authority of the past.[8] Indeed it is not too much of an exaggeration to say that market liberal policy delivers the *coup de grace* to practices of authority and of subscription to tradition already severely weakened during the modern period. Perhaps the most salient feature of our age is not a decline in individual liberty but the vanishing of authority, and a concomitant metamorphosis of moral judgements into a species of personal preferences, between which reason is powerless to arbitrate.[9] The tendency ency of market liberal policy is significantly to reinforce subjectivist and even antinomian tendencies which are already very powerful in modernist societies and thereby to render surviving enclaves and remnants of traditional life powerless before them.

The Old Right project of cultural fundamentalism is best understood as an ill-thought-out response to the modern dissolution of old forms of moral life that contemporary conservative policy has itself promoted or accelerated. This is not to say that all such older forms of community and moral life lacked value. On the contrary, the reactionary perception of cultural loss as a real historical phenomenon is sometimes well-founded, and it is singularly lacking among contemporary conservatives; but that does not mean that the old forms of life can, or even should, be reconstituted. The current conservative clamour about family breakdown is not only dishonest in repressing the role that market-driven economic changes — sometimes occurring over several generations, but greatly accelerated in recent years, as with female participation in the workforce — have played in transforming family life. It is also self-deceiving in imagining that older forms of family life can conceivably be revived in which modern Western demands for choice and self-fulfilment — which are in other areas elevated by conservatives to the status of fetishes — are denied. The current neo-fundamentalist clamour for a return to the traditional family is, in other words, misconceived and frivolous in the highest degree. It expresses no serious concern for the needs of people in families, nor any understanding of the diverse forms in which the institution of the family is now to be found. Such vulgar clamour is symptomatic of contemporary conservative thought in the unreality of its perception of real people and their needs. The adoption by Conservative governments of a neo-fundamentalist stance on family policy is best understood as an act of desperation, reinforced by the remoteness from public sentiment bred by the hermetic culture of the new Tory *nomenklatura*. Its political effect will be to speed Conservatives along the road to electoral oblivion.

The Political Economy Of Erewhon: The Market Liberal Utopia

The desolation of settled communities and the ruin of established expectations will not be mourned and may well be welcomed by fundamentalist market liberals. For them, nothing much of any value is threatened by the unfettered operation of market institutions. Communities and ways of life which cannot renew themselves through the exercise of consumer choice deserve to perish. The protection from market forces of valuable cultural forms is a form of unacceptable paternalism. And so the familiar and tedious litany goes on.

Underlying this fundamentalist conception of market institutions is a model of society that in its rationalistic utopianism and its hubristic doctrine of global convergence on a universal civilisation resembles nothing more closely than the most primitive forms of classical Marxism. Classical liberalism, or what I have termed market fundamentalism, is, like Marxism, a variation on the Enlightenment project, which is the project of transcending the contingencies of history and cultural difference and founding a universal civilisation that is qualitatively different from any that has ever before existed. The conflict between fundamentalist liberalism and the European tradition of conservative thought is plain and incontrovertible, if only in the fact that conservatives as different as Burke and de Maistre defined their outlook in terms of enmity towards the central project of the Enlightenment. It was left to the conservatives of the late twentieth century to yoke conservatism, perhaps for the first time in its history, to an Enlightenment utopia. If, as I believe, we are now in circumstances in which conservative philosophy can no longer give us much guidance, this is partly because we live in a post-Enlightenment age, an age in which the best thought views the Enlightenment from a perspective of historical distance rather than setting itself in opposition to it. This is to say that we view the European Enlightenment, like the Renaissance and the Reformation, as a cultural transformation that has left permanent marks on all subsequent thought and practice that cannot be reversed. Nor, equally, can we found policy on Enlightenment expectations — of convergence on a universal civilisation, and of progress in the growth of knowledge occurring in tandem with increasing human emancipation — which the historical experience of our century, and of mankind generally, renders incredible. Although it has transformed our cultures irreversibly, the Enlightenment cannot be for us — what it was for the French *philosophes*, and perhaps still is for a few Old Believers in America — an *ersatz* religion. Our situation, as late moderns, whether we wish it or not, is to belong to a post-Enlightenment culture, in which the rationalist religions of humanity are as almost as archaic, as alien and as remote as the traditional transcendental faiths. It is therefore deeply ironic that conservatism should have surrendered its scepticism in regard to the Enlightenment at just the historical moment at which the Enlightenment project should be everywhere in evident disarray or actual collapse.

The kinship of market fundamentalism with classical Marxism is evident in at least three respects. Both are forms of *economism* in that their model of man is that of *homo economicus* and they theorise cultural and political life in the reductionist terms of economic determinism. A *reductio ad absurdum* of the reductionist analysis of social life on the basis of an abstract and in fact *a priori* model of market exchange may be found in the works of the Chicago economist Gary Becker, but less extreme versions of the same approach are to be found in the application of economic analysis to political and bureaucratic behaviour.[10] Secondly, this form of economic imperialism involves a marginalisation of cultural difference in human life that grossly underestimates its political importance and even distorts our view of market institutions. It occludes our perception of political realities by treating nationalism and ethnic allegiance as ephemeral, and even epiphenomenal or derivative, episodes in modern life. It blunts our understanding of market institutions themselves by neglecting their cultural variability — a decisive mistake at any time, but especially momentous at present, when radically different East Asian market institutions are overtaking Occidental ones, particularly those of the Anglo-American varieties, on virtually any measure of performance. In general, it encourages the erroneous view of market institutions as free-standing entities, and the mistaken expectation that they will converge on a single model.[11] Thirdly, the economic imperialism of the fundamentalist conception of market institutions suggests a view of society, explicit in Hayek and before him in Herbert Spencer, in which it is nothing but a nexus of market exchanges, such that allegiance can be secured to a liberal political order that is universal and embodies no particular cultural tradition. In this paleo-liberal or libertarian view, the erosion of distinctive cultures by market processes is, if anything, to be welcomed as a sign of progress toward a universal rational civilisation. Here paleo-liberalism shows its affinities not with European conservatism but with the Old Left project of doing away with, or marginalising politically, the human inheritance of cultural difference.

That this perspective is a hallucinatory and utopian one is clear if we consider its neglect of the sources not only of political allegiance but also of social order in common cultural forms. Market liberalism, like other Enlightenment ideologies, treats cultural difference as a politically marginal phenomenon whose appropriate sphere is in private life. It does not comprehend, or repudiates as irrationality, the role of a common culture in sustaining political order and in legitimating market institutions. It maintains that only a regime of common rules, perhaps embodying a shared conception of rights, is required for the stability of market institutions and of a liberal civil society. This species of *liberal legalism* overlooks, or denies, that market institutions will not be politically stable — at any rate when they are combined with democratic institutions — if they do not accord with widespread conceptions of fairness, if they violate other important cultural norms, or if they have too destructive an effect on established expectations. In short, they deny the evident facts that the wholly free market is incompatible with social and political stability, while the stability of market institutions themselves depends far more on their political and cultural acceptability than upon the legal framework which supposedly defines and protects them.

Market liberal responses to this criticism fall into two categories — the ideological and the pragmatic. Market liberal ideologists will argue that the stability of a market society is only a matter of enforcing its laws. This thoroughly foolish reply need not detain us. It neglects the political fragility of the rule of law, and the frequent impossibility of enforcing it — points market liberals seem able to grasp in the context of laws which flout supply and demand, such as price controls, but which they appear incapable of generalising. The pragmatic market liberal response is to argue that market institutions need no legitimation so long as they deliver the goods in terms of general prosperity. This argument is illuminating in that it reveals the dependency of market liberal thought on the permanent possibility of rapid and continuous economic growth. It shows also that market liberalism has few sources of legitimacy on which to call when market economies go through a bad patch. It is the dim or unspoken recognition of this problem of legitimation for market institutions in times of poor economic performance that has led many market fundamentalists to compromise the rationalist purity of their doctrine and to combine it with varieties of moral or cultural fundamentalism.

Market liberalism is a utopian ideology in that the free market institutions to which it is devoted cannot in the real world of human history be combined with social or political stability. (This result is corroborated rather than undermined by the American example, in which a highly individualist ideal of market institutions has been rendered compatible with social stability only by the adoption of protectionist and regulatory policies more restrictive and far-reaching than those of almost any other Western country.) It is utopian in its view of market institutions themselves — as perpetual motion machines requiring only a legal framework and government non-interference to deliver uninterrupted growth — and in its refusal to accept that sometimes an active macro-economic policy is necessary to keep a market economy on an even keel. It is utopian in its neglect, or denial, of the truth that market institutions are stable when, and only when, they come embedded in cultural forms which constrain and inform their workings.

Market liberalism is at its most utopian, however, in its conception of a global market society, in which goods, and perhaps people, move freely between economies having radically different stages of development and harbouring very different cultures. Global free trade, as it is envisaged by economic liberals and embodied in the GATT agreements of late 1993, will subject both developing and mature economies to levels of strain and job dislocation severer than they have ever before known. The displacement of peasants in hitherto agrarian economies and of industrial workers in Europe by an untrammelled global market will unavoidably have consequences for the social and political stability of both kinds of economies that have not been addressed in the Panglossian scenarios of the supporters of world-wide free trade.[12] In

Europe, the politically destabilising effects of structural unemployment in excess of ten percent are already visible in electoral support for renascent radical parties of the Right; it does not need powers of clairvoyance to divine the political impact of further large job losses arising from an influx of goods produced at around one tenth of European labour costs. Nor does it require more than a smattering of knowledge of twentieth century history to guess what are likely to be the results of attempting to force on European peoples a structural economic adjustment larger, deeper and quicker, than any they have yet suffered other than as a consequence of war. Supporters of global free trade do not confront its systemic effects on the stability of families and communities. Global free trade imposes an inexorable downward pressure on workers' incomes in the First World for a variety of reasons, including demographic reasons. Further, it dislocates settled communal life by imposing unending job mobility on workers and their families. As Herman Daly has written: 'Given the existing overpopulation and high demographic growth of the Third World it is clear that equalisation (of incomes) will be downward, as it has indeed been during the last decade in the US ... Even with uniformly high wages made possible by universal population control and redistribution, and with uniform internalization of external costs, free trade and free capital mobility still increase the separation of ownership and control and the forced mobility of labour which are so inimical to community.'[13] These destabilising effects of global free trade are not incidental but integral to it.

The political frivolity of the utopia of a frontierless global market of the sort that is embodied in the GATT agreements is perhaps only matched by that of proposals for the European Union that envisage a continental labour market operating under a single transnational currency. Such proposals for an unfettered single European market neglect not only the vast differences in economic development within the EU but also the embeddedness of the diverse market institutions that the EU harbours in divergent national cultures. At the same time, the project of a single European currency is bound to result in great stagnant pools of unemployment, regional and even national in scope, if it is not combined with an effective transnational labour market. Such a market has no precedent in modern history and there can be little doubt that the attempt to impose it will encounter a powerful political backlash. In general, attempts to steam-roller the European peoples into an artificial and culturally disembedded single market can only work to strengthen political support for nationalism. Such a reinforcement of nationalism in Europe, arising from insensitivity to national cultures, can only have the effect of making more difficult those forms of European cooperation — on a common defence and foreign policy, for example — that Europe's present circumstances make desirable and indeed urgently necessary.

Both visions, for GATT and for a federalist European Union, are Neo-Liberal rationalist utopias that will founder on the reefs of history and human nature, with costs in human suffering that may come to rival those of twentieth century experiments in central economic planning. These and other similarly utopian projects of market liberalism neglect enduring needs of human beings an understanding of which was once preserved in conservative thought. Human beings need, more than they need the freedom of consumer choice, a cultural and economic environment that offers them an acceptable level of security and in which they feel at home. Market institutions that deny this need will be politically repudiated. The project of constructing a market liberal utopia in which these needs for security and common life are not met has as its only sure outcome the spawning of atavistic movements that wreak havoc on the historic inheritance of liberal institutions. The challenge for thought and policy is that of abandoning once for all the project of any such utopia and of applying the genuine insights of conservative thought to the novel circumstances in which we find ourselves. The results of this intellectual enterprise are bound to be radical and — for conventional Western conservatives — unacceptable.

What Conservatism Was

A central theme of this inquiry is that, partly because of the novelty of the times and partly because it has abandoned its most distinctive insights and concerns, conservatism may no longer for us be a viable political outlook. Conservative thought may well not be alone in suffering obsolescence and redundancy at this juncture in history, since it is plausible that both socialist thought, and the standard forms of liberalism, face a similar superannuation. In each of these traditions of thought there are insights that can and should be salvaged from the wreckage, but my aim here is to identify those grains of truth in conservative thought that retain a lasting value even as conservatism itself shuffles off the scene.

As it is expressed in such twentieth century writers as Oakeshott and Santayana,[14] say a conservative outlook on society and government encompassed three themes that are salient to our current circumstance and which are denied, or little understood, in the presently dominant schools of free market conservatism. There is first the belief that human beings as we find them are not individual specimens of generic humanity but practitioners of particular cultures. It is from these cultures that they derive their identities, which are never that of universal humanity, but rather those conferred by the particular, and unchosen, inheritances of history and language. What is most essential about us, accordingly, is what is most accidental, and what makes each of us what he is a local and not a universal matter.[15] Indeed, in this conservative view the very meaning of anyone's life is a matter of local knowledge, and the greatest disaster that can befall any community is that the shared understandings — the myths, rituals and narratives — that confer meaning on the lives of its participants be dissipated in too rapid or too sweeping cultural change. 'The Masai, when they were moved from their old country to the present Masai reserve in Kenya, took with them the names of their hills and plains and rivers and gave them to the hills and plains and rivers of the new country. And it is by some such subterfuge of conservatism that every man or people compelled to suffer a notable change avoids the shame of extinction.'[16] It was by such a subterfuge that the shamanists of Lake Baikal, forbidden to worship their old gods by the Soviet communist regime, renamed them after the Paris Communards, thereby preserving from extinction both their religion and their very identity.[17]

The conservation of local knowledge, because such knowledge is constitutive of our very identity, is a central value in any outlook that is truly conservative. Local knowledge is threatened, or destroyed, by economic or cultural changes that are large and incessant. It is by now recognised that agricultural collectivisation in Soviet Russia and the Ukraine resulted not only in millions of deaths but in a loss of the practical knowledge of farmers, and a destruction of peasant cultural traditions, that are irreversible. Less commonly perceived is the loss of local knowledge that comes about through constant business reorganisation, ephemeral job tenure, and unremitting mobility of labour, which are forced on contemporary societies by unrestricted market competition. There is a real paradox here, one that has gone wholly unremarked in the banal discourse of recent conservatism, in that the epistemic argument for market institutions, which rightly stresses their superiority over planning institutions in utilising dispersed local knowledge, must be supplemented by the observation that unfettered markets tend to destroy or dissipate local knowledge. They do so by rendering local knowledge increasingly obsolete or irrelevant to the operation of market processes that are themselves ever more disembedded. If, as I am inclined to think, conservatism is best stated not as a moral but as an epistemic doctrine — as the doctrine that the knowledge that is most important in the lives of human beings is local, practical, traditional and, as Edward Goldsmith has reminded us, ineffable[18] — then contemporary conservatism founders on the contradiction that it has committed itself to the hegemony of market institutions whose workings render traditional human knowledge worthless and the social world unintelligible in its terms.

A fundamental objection to the paleo-liberal regime of incessant economic change under unfettered market institutions, then, is that in devaluing traditional knowledge it renders social and economic life ever less understandable to its human participants. In so doing, unfettered market institutions tend to deplete the cultural identities of their practitioners — upon which these institutions themselves depend. Market institutions will enhance human well-being, and will be stably renewed across the generations, when they do not go against the grain of the particular cultures that harbour them, but on the contrary assist those cultures to reproduce themselves. By imposing on people a regime of incessant change and permanent revolution, unencumbered market institutions deplete the stock of historical memory on which cultural identity depends. The common cliché that globalised markets tend to yield cultural uniformity is therefore not without an element of truth. What such cultural homogenisation signifies is perhaps less obvious: a breach in historical memory which disrupts, or empties of significance, the narratives in terms of which people make sense of their lives. If, as any conservative who is also a sceptic is bound to think, the meaning of life for all of us is a local matter, this junking of local knowledge by unencumbered market processes is no small matter. For these and similar reasons, the loss of historical memory brought about by globalised market forces will be recognised — on any view that is authentically conservative, or for that matter reflectively liberal — as a form of cultural impoverishment, not a stage on the way to a universal civilisation. Let us call this first conservative belief *anti-universalism*, which is the insight that cultural difference belongs to the human essence, and its concomitant, the perception that the identities of human beings depend on the renewal of the particular cultural forms by which they are constituted.

A second conservative theme is what I shall call *non-progress*, or anti-meliorism. By this I mean the conservative rejection of the idea of indefinite world-improvement as either a realistic or a desirable end of political life. It is common among conservative thinkers to stress the Augustinian insight that, like all things human, political institutions are imperfect and imperfectible, so that the project of a *political providence* which promises to deliver mankind from mystery and tragedy — which was the project of Marxism-Leninism — is at once impious (from the standpoint of any religious believer) and impossible. The perception of human imperfectibility is, however, only one, and not in the end perhaps the most important, reason why a conservative will reject the idea of progress, at least as an animating idea in political and economic life. He will reject it because it presupposes a uniform standard of evaluation and improvement of human life, whereas it is an implication of his first belief that, limiting cases aside, such standards will vary across different cultures. If the bottom line in political and moral reasoning is a conception of human well-being, and if human well-being is bound up with participation in common cultural forms whose content varies to a significant degree, then there will except in limiting cases be no common measure for improvement in different cultures. It is not then the possibility of global betterment that the conservative rejects so much as its meaningfulness.

Finally, for a conservative there is surely something anomalous in making progress rather than the sustainability or stability of society the end of political life. Any decent society will do what it can to alleviate the unavoidable misfortunes of human life, to enable and empower its members in coping with them and to ensure those that cannot be avoided can nevertheless be borne with dignity and consolation. The politics of open-ended improvement, however, was, and is, or — should be — alien to a conservative sensibility. Such a melioristic approach to human life cannot help encouraging unreal hopes of the human future and distracting us from dealing with the minute particulars of our lives as they are now. 'We all feel at this time the ambiguity of mechanical progress. It seems to multiply opportunity, but it destroys the possibility of simple, rural or independent life. It lavishes information, but it abolishes mastery except in trivial or mechanical efficiency. We learn many languages, but we degrade our own. Our philosophy is highly critical and thinks itself enlightened, but it is a Babel of mutually unintelligible artificial tongues.'[19] And the idea of indefinite progress is easily associated with the notion that social dilemmas are soluble by the generation of ever more resources through economic growth. This association is not a necessary or inevitable one, as we can see from the example of JS Mill, who insisted that a stationary state need not be one in which human improvement has come to a halt;[20] But it is a common one which contemporary conservative thought does nothing to question. The fact is that in conservative thought, as we know it today,[21] a vulgar and unreflective meliorism about the human prospect is combined with a crudely economistic conception of what social improvement consists in. It is not from this thin gruel that we can hope for sustenance.

The third element in a conservative outlook I shall call *the primacy of cultural forms*, or anti-reductionism. By this I mean the idea, implied by much that has gone before, that neither market institutions nor political institutions can or should be autonomous in regard to the cultures they serve. Rather, they are themselves to be assessed, and controlled, by reference to the ends and norms of the cultures in which they are embedded. Market institutions which have been disembedded from their underlying cultures may increase the output of goods and services but they will not enhance human well-being through their activities.[22] Again the idea that there is, or could be, a single model for market institutions is to be rejected, since they will properly vary according to their cultural matrices and social contexts. In this conservative view, the disembedding of market institutions from their parent cultures, and the conferring on them of functional autonomy, is one of the disasters of modern societies, since it amounts to a severance of markets from the ends they appropriately serve. The denial of the primacy of cultural forms is, of course, an implication of any Neo-Liberal view that makes a fetish of consumer choice, and of any more developed liberal philosophy which accords an intrinsic value to choice-making independently of the goodness of that which is chosen. And it is a necessary presupposition of the knee-jerk response of economic liberals which regards all political intervention in economic life as an evil that stands in need of justification.

The deeper import of the idea of the primacy of cultural forms is that it is not through the activity of choice-making that values are created in our lives. The conception of the autonomous human subject, though it is a central one in contemporary liberal thought, and one which I have myself deployed in earlier work,[23] easily degenerates into a dangerous fiction. In its common uses, the idea of autonomy neglects the central role in human life of chance and fate — of the unchosen accidents that confer our identities on us and the further accidents that befall us in life that choice has no part in and, where they are misfortunes, can do little or nothing to remedy. And it sanctifies that fiction of liberal philosophy, the fiction of the unsituated human subject, which is author of its ends and creator of the values in its life. It is, indeed, this liberal fiction whose emaciated ghost stalks the dim ruins of paleo-liberal ideology, gibbering of global markets and economic efficiency.

In the subtlest liberal uses of the idea of autonomy, it is recognised that the exercise of autonomous choice depends for its value on a cultural environment that is rich in choiceworthy options and inherently public goods.[24] In this subtler liberal perspective, value is not an artefact of individual choice, it is discovered rather than created by us, and what has value in our lives is often far from transparent to us.[25] It is arguable, and plausible, that even this subtler liberal conception of autonomy unreasonably privileges a particular Western ideal, whose costs and illusions it has not fully perceived.[26] From the standpoint being developed in this paper, the ideal of autonomy has the clear danger of reinforcing the excesses of individualism promoted in Neo-Liberal thought and policy by further undervaluing the human need for common forms of life. All that is of value in the subtler liberal conception of autonomy can be captured, without the excesses of individualism, in the ideas of independence and enablement, where the human subjects that are so enabled are not the noumenal fictions of liberal theory but flesh and blood practitioners of particular, historically constituted forms of life. It is with the enablement of human beings as they are in the real world of history and practice, embedded in their specific and diverse cultures, traditions and communities, rather than with the rights of the empty ciphers of liberal theory, that political thought and public policy ought rightly to be concerned. Such concerns are only obfuscated by the shallow discourse of choice and rights that has dominated British life for the last decade and more.

After Conservatism

The conservative idea of the primacy of cultural forms is meant to displace not only standard liberal conceptions of the autonomous human subject but also ideas of the autonomy of market institutions that liberal thought has recently been applied — or misapplied — to support. It is not meant to support paleo-conservative and reactionary conceptions of organic or integral community which have no application in our historical circumstances and which, if they were implemented politically, could end only in tragedy or — more likely in Britain — black comedy. The idea of a seamless community — the *noumenal community*, as we may call it, of recent communitarianism[27] — is as much of a fiction as the autonomous subject of liberal theory. We all of us belong to many communities, we mostly inherit diverse ethnicities, and our world-views are fractured and provisional whether or not we know it or admit it. We harbour a deep diversity of views and values as to sexuality and the worth of human life, our relations with the natural environment and the special place, if any, of the human species in the scheme of things. The reactionary project of rolling back this diversity of values and world-views in the pursuit of a lost cultural unity[28] overlooks the character of our cultural inheritance as a palimpsest, having ever deeper layers of complexity.

Those who imagine that diversity and uncertainty of world-view are confined to the chattering classes are themselves captivated by the constructions of their own discourse. The healthy, unreflective folk culture of their imagination corresponds to nothing in common life; and the assertion of robust common sense against the depredations of 'theorists' and opinion-formers is itself made ridiculous by the bookish ignorance it displays. Among us, High Toryism can only be a pose, a playful or frivolous distraction from serious political reflection in a world in which authority and tradition are barely memories. Indeed, contemporary paleo-conservatives are reminiscent of no one so much as Joseph de Maistre, who set off for Russia in the hope of finding a people not 'scribbled on' by *philosophes*, only to discover a culture of Francophiles. For us a common culture cannot — and, for anyone touched by a liberal sensibility, should not — be a seamless web. It must consist of what the diverse traditions that our society harbours can recognise as a shared inheritance, which will reasonably change over time. The liberal legalist view and the reactionary or organicist view are equally removed from the realities and needs of our current circumstances. The effect of market liberalism has been to run down our common stock of cultural traditions by propagating the absurd liberal legalist view that we do not need a common culture but only common rules, while the patent failings of this paleo-liberal view have inspired the vain attempt to recapture a lost cultural unity. Cultural fundamentalism has emerged in a vain attempt to shore up the tottering edifice of market fundamentalism. Neither conservative position seriously answers to our present needs.

There is a contemporary conservative view — somewhat distinct from any reactionary or organicist posture, and argued in its most appealing and persuasive form by David Willetts[29] — that holds that the disruptive effects of unfettered market institutions on the lives of communities have been much exaggerated. It is probably not an unfair caricature of this position to say that it is confident that in conditions of steady economic growth communities are pretty robust and can in most things safely be left to their own devices. It is hard to see what in contemporary conditions justifies such confidence. It may be true that communities were able to renew themselves in circumstances of rapid economic change in England in the latter part of the nineteenth century, say, but such circumstances cannot be replicated now. At that time, much of the English working class was subject to the influence of nonconformist Christianity, with all the restraints on behaviour that that implied, including a form of family life in which duty and commitment had priority over self-realisation and romantic love. Personal behaviour was subject to a level of social monitoring, to norms of respectability and to sanctions of ostracism and stigma that are unknown among us. Both neighbourhoods and churches were small, slow-moving face to face societies in which such sanctions were real and telling. None of these conditions obtains in Britain today or will exist in any realistically foreseeable future. They have been destroyed by a century and more of social changes which market liberal policies have only accelerated and deepened. Most of Britain is a post-religious, and in particular a post-Christian society, for good or ill, and the culture of marriage and the family is permeated by ideals of choice and self-fulfilment of the sorts celebrated by latter-day defenders of the free market. And, as I have noted, the fragmentation of family life which contemporary conservatives bemoan is, in very large part, a product of the culture of choice, and the economy of unfettered mobility, which they themselves celebrate.

It may be that the best prospects for traditional conservative values are to be found today not in any Occidental country but in the East Asian cultures. The absence, or weakness, in these cultures of the romantic and individualist conception of married life that characterises Western bourgeois societies, and which are at their strongest in those societies, such as American society, in which family breakdown is most pervasive and extreme, may well go a long way toward accounting for their extraordinary economic achievements. It is ironical that the East Asian societies, which have been more successful than most Occidental countries in combining dynamic market institutions with stable communities, should have been so little studied by Western conservatives. No-one imagines that the successes of the East Asian countries can be replicated in the very different cultural and historical milieux in which we find ourselves in Europe today. It is nevertheless a reflection on the poverty of Western conservatism that it should have failed to reflect on the experience of countries that have been more successful than any Western country in finding and maintaining the elusive balance between the claims of individual choice and the human need for a life in common.

For us, in Britain today, individualism and pluralism are an historical fate. We may reasonably hope to temper this fate, and thereby to make the best of the opportunities it offers us; we cannot hope to escape it. Yet it is just such an escape from our historical fate that is promised by those conservatives who seek answers to our social problems in the revival of religious and moral beliefs and disciplines — 'Victorian values' — that vanished generations ago. It is idle and silly to imagine that the resources of self-discipline, or the forms of social monitoring, exist among us which sustained the deferral of gratification among the mid-Victorians. The close neighbourhoods of Victorian times have been dissolved by the demands of labour mobility. Family life has changed utterly with contraception and the increased, and sometimes predominant role of married women in the provision of the family income. Nor are these changes necessarily, or in fact, by any means all for the bad. The point is that they remove many of the resources whereby mid-nineteenth century communities renewed themselves in the face of rapid economic change. It is hard to understand the confidence of those who believe that communities without these resources will succeed in adapting to the impact of economic changes powered by far greater, and far more swiftly moving, global market forces.

Such confidence arises, in all probability, from a failure to perceive that the requirements of unfettered market institutions and those of stable communities may and do come into deep conflict. It expresses also, no doubt, resistance to the policy implication of such a perception, which is that communities need shelter from the gale of market competition, else they will be scattered to the winds. In the last resort, this contemporary conservative view regards communities as adjuncts to markets, optional extras in a society of market exchanges, rather than the sources of the needs markets exist to serve. It can therefore never accept that markets may need to be constrained, or channelled, so as to meet the needs of communities. For constraints on markets will presumably entail losses of efficiency, and so of output. And any loss of output, particularly if it is produced by political intervention aiming to protect something as elusive as the stability of a community, must be an error in policy. This contemporary conservative view is in the end, accordingly, a variation on a familiar theme of market liberalism, which is that market institutions are justified as engines of economic growth. The argument of this paper, however, is that — as Aristotle anciently observed — economic activity is senseless unless it satisfies human needs. It is this old and homely truth that the new conservatism, even in its most intelligent forms, seems to have determinedly forgotten.

New Measures For Conserving Common Life

All strands of conventional political and economic thought are at one in staking our future on a continuation of economic growth as we have hitherto known it. They all thereby commit themselves to a political version of Pascal's wager — itself a celebratedly bad bet. It would seem more prudent to think and plan on the assumption that the common fate of the mature economies, at any rate — the economies of Western Europe and Japan, for example — is low economic growth, and to begin to consider how social and political life may best be organised when — doubtless willy-nilly rather than by any kind of premeditated policy — we find ourselves landed in something akin to a stationary state economy. The problems of legitimating market institutions in a context in which no-one can expect that his or her income or living standards will rise automatically have as yet hardly begun to be discussed.

The dilemmas opened up by the prospect of a near-stationary economy are not only political ones. The promise of an open horizon of growth and of an indefinite improvement in the human lot have served as a surrogate for religious conviction in an age in which the great *political* fact is the passing of Christianity. An inexorable consequence of the passing of Christianity — understood here not as a variety of personal faith but as the unifying world-view of a culture — is the waning of the secular religions of progress and humanity in which Christian moral hopes found political expression. The cultural void that yawns when the secular meliorism of the religion of growth founders is as yet too far away to be on any intellectual or political agenda. If it is thought of at all, it is as an element in a fundamentalist project for the rechristianisation of Western societies which can be taken seriously by no one with any sense of historical perspective. The question of what is to be the content of the common culture in a country such as Britain, when it is no longer animated by inherited transcendental faith or by any variety of the Enlightenment project, is a deep and difficult one that I cannot consider here. It is clear only that, for us at any rate, a common culture cannot mean a common world-view, religious or secular. It is an implication of all that I have said, however, that we have no option but to struggle to make our inheritance of liberal traditions work. At present, the principal obstacle we face in the struggle to renew our inheritance of liberal practice is the burden on thought and policy of market liberal dogma.

Liberal dogmas work to occlude our perception of the dangers to liberal society arising from current policies. They dim our vision, most particularly, of the dangers to social and political stability arising from the ever greater autonomy of market institutions. Little serious thought has yet been given, for example, to the problems arising from the combination of a near stationary state economy with rapidly ongoing technological innovation which market institutions are producing in most, if not all, of the world's mature economies. This is a combination whose difficulties John Stuart Mill, writing on the stationary state in the mid-nineteenth century, could hardly be expected to anticipate. The central difficulty is that the enlargement of leisure that Mill, by contrast with the gloomier classical economists, expected to come from stability in population and output against a background of improvement in the industrial arts is occurring in the form of ever higher levels of involuntary unemployment. There can be little doubt that for the medium to longer term the agenda for thought is that of redefining full employment as a policy objective in terms that do not mean full-time jobs in an expanding economy. It may be that proposals for a basic or citizen's income, where that is to be distinguished from the Neo-Liberal idea of a negative income tax, and for a better distribution of capital among the citizenry, need reconsideration — despite all their difficulties — as elements in a policy aiming to reconcile the human need for economic security with the destabilising dynamism of market institutions.[30] Even the outlines of a policy for such a new pattern of full employment, however, are as yet barely visible to us.

We can nevertheless be reasonably sure that the difficult transition to this new order of things will be made impossible if the relentless elimination of jobs by advancing technology is compounded by the job-destroying effects in the mature economies of global free trade. The proposition that Western labour forces can or must adapt to a global labour market in which their competitors earn a tenth of their wages is not one that commends itself either to good sense or political prudence. Nor is global free trade forced on us by anything in the Ricardian theory of comparative advantage, since a regional free trade area such as the EEA is already larger than any that has ever before existed in human history and is diverse enough to satisfy all the Ricardian requirements. Indeed it is far from clear that Ricardian theory demands, or even supports, global free trade. Ricardo himself had doubts about the idea of comparative advantage, especially when it involves the technology-driven displacement of labour, that seem to have eluded his latter-day disciples. In Chapter 31 of his *Principles of Political Economy and Taxation* entitled ' On Machinery', Ricardo states that 'I am convinced that the substitution of machinery for human labour is often very injurious to the interests of the class of labourers.' Ricardo goes on: ' ... the discovery and use of machinery may be attended with a diminution of gross produce; and whenever that is the case, it will be injurious to the labouring class, as some of their number will be thrown out of employment, and population will become redundant compared with the funds which are to employ it.' Ricardo concludes: ' ... the opinion entertained by the labouring class, that the employment of machinery is frequently detrimental to their interests, is not founded on prejudice and error, but is conformable to the correct principles of political economy.'[31] It is fair to surmise that the force of Ricardo's doubts could only have been increased in a circumstance, such as ours, in which an untramelled global market in labour-saving technologies is envisaged and on the way to implementation through the GATT agreements. It is, indeed, a circumstance of just such a sort — in which employers make productivity and profitability gains at the cost of unemployment and reduced incomes for workers — that Ricardo envisaged. For his followers, by contrast, the benefits of free trade are *a priori* truths, which mere observation cannot hope to bring into question.

On presently observable evidence, the likely result of the GATT agreements, if they are ever implemented, is not only ruin for Third World agriculture, with a billion or more peasants being displaced from the land in the space of a generation or less, but — as Sir James Goldsmith has warned[32] — class war in the advanced countries as wages fall and the return on offshore capital rises. It defies both common sense and historical experience to suppose that the economic and social dislocations produced by exposure to a global market larger, more dynamic and more uneven in development than any that has ever before existed can be absorbed by reductions in wages and shifts of manpower on a scale and at a rate that are wholly unprecedented, without a political backlash emerging in response to the devastating impact of this process of structural adjustment on working-class living standards. Such a backlash is made all the more likely given that this adjustment is demanded of working people at precisely the time when much of the social protection embodied in the postwar welfare state is being dismantled. In this historical context, global free trade is a recipe for social conflict and political instability on a large scale. A prerequisite for any policy that can hope to offer a decent measure of economic security to the population is accordingly an urgent reconsideration of the market liberal dogma of global free trade.

Market liberal policy is harmful to settled communities in many other areas. Policy in regard to cities has in Britain been grotesquely poor, with their deformation as communities by the private motor car, and their hollowing out by such developments as warehouse shopping being particularly unacceptable examples. Here the culprit is not primarily the influence of special interests, important though that undoubtedly has been, but rather Neo-Liberal blindness to the city itself as an institution and a form of life that is worthy of preservation and renewal. Cities — at least as these have been understood hitherto in the European tradition to which Britain belongs — are not congeries of strangers. They are not nomadic encampments, traffic islands or ephemeral aggregates of enterprises and households. They are long-standing human settlements, spanning the generations, whose welfare can neither be understood nor assured as an upshot of a myriad unco-ordinated private decisions. Protecting cities as human settlements demands institutions for accountability and planning, devolved as far as is feasible and appropriate, which are anathema to Neo-Liberal dogma. This is only one example, but a vitally important one, of the way in which conservative policy cast in a Neo-Liberal mould has been inimical to the conservation of precious cultural achievements and forms of common life.

It is not my intention to try here to address the whole range of policy issues in which market liberal thinking has led us astray.[33] The key alterations in thought that must precede any such detailed re-examination of policy are scrapping the conception of market institutions as perpetual motion machines for economic growth and abandoning indefinite growth in output as a sensible objective of human effort. This is not to say that growth must be replaced as an objective by no growth. That would be hardly less nonsensical, since economic growth is itself a statistical abstraction that takes no account of the contribution to human well-being of the activities it purportedly measures. What it means rather is that economic activity is not an end in itself but must serve the needs and values of the cultures in which it is pursued. It must be sustainable in its longer-term impact on both the natural and the human environments, at least in the weak sense that it does not result in their irreversible degradation. And it must be sustainable in the stronger sense that it fosters, instead of undermining, stability in the communities it affects. Of course, stability is not fixity, and we cannot put the genie of technological virtuosity back into the bottle. But this is only to say that economic change is continuous and unavoidable and must therefore be channelled, not that it can be let to run its course with the devil taking the hindmost.

Such channelling of unavoidable economic change is unlikely to be successful so long as public policy and indeed the public culture are animated by the idea of the insatiability of ever-expanding human wants. I have argued elsewhere that a conception of satiable human needs has a central role in reasoned discourse about public policy.[34] The idea of a satiable human need will be workable in public discourse, however, only if the ruling ideal of the unending proliferation of human wants is relinquished and replaced by a conception of *sufficiency* in which it is the quality of social life, rather than the quantity of goods and services, that is the central objective of public policy. One of the themes of this paper is that political parties in Britain and similar countries have been slow to recognise that, in conditions of low economic growth, political discourse is bound to focus increasingly on quality-of-life issues. A connected point is that, once we no longer expect or hope for a resumption of economic growth that can allow a return to full employment as that has conventionally been understood, we are free to consider how new forms of livelihood can be developed to supplement, or replace, older forms of job-holding. What is particularly important to note here is that the pursuit of sufficiency, in the context of providing people with opportunities for fulfilling livelihood and elsewhere, presupposes that market institutions be subject to political constraints. We have no hope of achieving fulfilling livelihood for all in the context of technology-driven displacement of labour by global free trade. The content of sufficiency, for any particular society at any particular time, must be a political judgement, arrived at by reasoned public discourse. Equally, the pursuit of sufficiency requires public policies in which the autonomy of market institutions is subordinated to political objectives of social stability and harmonious community.

Nothing advanced here is meant to cast doubt on the centrality and indispensability of market institutions in economic life. The point is that they must be harnessed and guided by political constraints if they are to serve human needs. Provided this condition is met, market institutions may well be extended in some areas of policy, where such extension helps to anchor institutions in local communities. There remains a good case for educational vouchers, not on the Neo-Liberal ground of promoting market competition, but on the ground that sensibly designed voucher schemes might render schools more sensitive than they are now to families and communities. Drawing on the ideas of Ivan Illich rather than upon Neo-Liberal thought, I have elsewhere advanced a version of an educational credit scheme in which it is not tied to any particular form of schooling and can be used by a diversity of institutions, traditions and communities.[35] A streamlined, or minimalist National Curriculum, could provide a common core of skills and knowledge as a standard for all families to meet, while they were otherwise free to meet the varying needs of their different communities. The details of such an educational credit scheme are less important than its objective, which is to harness market institutions to anchor schools, and other educational institutions, more securely in the communities they exist to serve. In some areas of welfare policy, also, voucher schemes can be defended as devices for devolving welfare institutions to the level closest to individuals, families and their communities. There are doubtless other, similar ways in which market institutions can be usefully extended. Such extension must always have the aim of embedding markets in the communities they serve and it must never concede to markets the autonomy and freedom from political constraint by which they have been privileged in Neo-Liberal theory.

Conclusion & Prospect

The conquest of conservative parties by Neo-Liberal ideology, and the embodiment of that ideology in public policy, have altered irreversibly the social and political landscape of countries such as Britain. In delegitimating traditional institutions, and confounding the expectations on which the lives of Conservative voters of all classes — but especially the middle classes — were based, Neo-Liberal policy has all but destroyed the social base of conservatism in Britain. A secular conservatism devoted to the protection of voters' economic interests — the only remotely plausible conservatism in a post-religious country such as Britain — has been taken off the political agenda for the foreseeable future by Tory policies which have ravaged and almost destroyed the traditional economic constituencies of British Conservatism. This undoing of conservatism by market liberalism is now an established fact of political life in Britain and in similarly placed countries. The likelihood that it augurs prolonged periods of electoral defeat for conservative governments and parties is, from the perspective of the present inquiry, less important than the exhaustion it betokens in conservative thought itself. That contingencies we cannot presently foresee will return Conservatives to government, at some time in the future, is a possibility that cannot definitively be excluded. Unlike the crazed Neo-Liberal ideologues of the Eighties, who pronounced that 'Labour will never rule again', we must never forget the phenomenon of chance in political life — the permanent political relevance of Cleopatra's nose — or neglect the related phenomenon of apparently deep-seated trends suddenly, and unpredictably, reversing themselves.

If, as I hazard the guess, the Conservatives face a long period of political marginality in Britain, conceivably lasting a generation, it could nevertheless be foreshortened considerably by errors and misfortunes occurring during a time of rule by the parties of the Left. It remains thoroughly unclear, however, what, if anything, a Conservative Government arising from failures in government on the Left would be devoted to conserving. The paradoxical likelihood is that — in Britain at any rate — the task of conserving, perhaps in altered forms, the best elements in our institutional inheritance will pass to parties which presently think of themselves as being on the Left. If supposed conservatives succumb to the pseudo-radicalism of free market ideology, then genuine conservatives have no option but to become true radicals. And, if ordinary people cannot find in the party of the Right concern for their security from crime, economic risk and the breakdown of community, they will turn elsewhere for it. In so doing they will only be giving electoral expression to what has long been a fact — that conservatism in Britain has lost any clear perception of what it is that ordinary people are most concerned to protect in their lives. It is the demise of any recognisable Tory philosophy, far more than the fatigue and loss of the will to rule produced by too long a spell in power, that best explains the electoral rout currently facing British Conservatism.

What Left and Right may mean in the coming years, and whether these terms will retain much usefulness, is not yet clear. What is unmistakably clear is that the intellectual hegemony in political life of the Right, as we used to understand it, is over. Moreover, it has become evident that conservative thought, lacking the intellectual resources needed to cope with the dilemmas thrown up by the conservative policies of the past decade or so, has in effect created the conditions for its own demise. Neither the conservative denial that the conflict between unfettered market institutions and stable communities is real, nor the reactionary project of recovering a vanished past, are sustainable responses to our predicament. Both, in their different ways, evade the real challenge of the post-socialist age, which is that of harnessing market institutions to the needs of stable communities and so giving liberal civilisation another lease on life.

The evident debility of conservative thought is only one sign of the obsolescence of the principal Western ideologies, which is mirrored in the ongoing melt-down, virtually world-wide, of the political and economic models which they sponsor. My focus here has been on the specious claims of paleo-liberal ideology, in which individual choice is elevated to the supreme value and at the same time emptied of all moral significance. Our present situation is the awkward one in which we can renew and extend liberal civilisation only insofar as we recognise its embeddedness in common forms of life unrecognised in liberal theory. It is unlikely that we will succeed in giving liberal society another lease on life if our intellectual outlook does not become — at least by the standards of recent liberal theorising — post-liberal. Within liberal thought, as within conservative thought, there are doubtless insights and truths that will survive the wreckage of liberal ideology; but the ruin of liberalism as an ideology is an undeniable fact of our present predicament. To the extent that as we accept this fact and thereby adopt a post-liberal perspective, we are bound to reject all those varieties of conservatism in which fundamentalist liberalism has found a political home.

An appropriate response to our present circumstance is a strategy of salvage and retrieval, of the kind attempted here with respect to the insights that have survived the wreckage of conservative philosophy. We will cope best with the new dilemmas we confront if we accept the undoing of conservatism and learn the lessons its undoing has to teach us. We may then be able to summon up the readiness to think afresh about a world in which conservative thought no longer gives us guidance or illumination.

NOTES & REFERENCES

1   F. A. Hayek, *The Constitution of Liberty*, Chicago: Chicago University Press, 1960, p. 41.

2   I have discussed some aspects of commercial expression in my monograph, *Advertising Bans: Administrative Decisions or Matters of Principle?*, London: Social Affairs Unit, 1991.

3   For a good statement of the contemporary New Left position, see Hilary Wainright, *Arguments for a New Left: Answering the Free Market Right*, Oxford and Cambridge Mass. : Blackwell, 1994.

4   I refer, of course, to Michael Oakeshott, and in particular to his essay, 'On being conservative', in *Rationalism in Politics and other Essays*, Indianapolis: Liberty Press.

5   Edward Luttwak, 'Why Fascism is the Wave of the Future', in *London Review of Books*, 7 April, 1994, pp. 3,6.

6   Adam Smith, *Lectures on Jurisprudence*, Indianapolis: Liberty Classics, 1982, pp. 539-540.

7   Ibid., p.541.

8   This is a point, made in regard primarily to British working-class communities, by Jeremy Seabrook in *Revolt against Change*.

9   The claim that it is the disappearance of authority that is the defining feature of the modern age is made by Hannah Arendt, and echoed by Alasdair MacIntyre, who adds the important rider that in a world without authority technical and managerial expertise will serve as its surrogate. See H. Arendt, *Between Past and Present*, and Alasdair MacIntyre, *After Virtue*. He might have further noted that medical and therapeutic discourse tends to displace moral judgement and practice. On this last point, see Philip Rieff, *The Triumph of the Therapeutic*.

10 In the subtlest versions of this approach, of which that of James Buchanan is pre-eminent, the drastic simplification involved in the adoption of the *homo economicus* model of political behaviour is candidly acknowledged. The epistemology underlying this view is clearly instrumentalist or pragmatist. On

Buchanan's work, see my 'Buchanan on liberty' in my *Post-liberalism: studies in political thought*, Routledge: London and New York, 1991.

11 These errors have been particularly debilitating in regard to thought and policy in regard to the post-communist societies. On this, see my *Post-Communist Societies in Transition: A Social Market Perspective*, Social Market Foundation, London, 1994.

12 See Sir James Goldsmith, *The Times*, March 5, 1994, for a masterly demolition of the usual arguments for global free trade, and a timely warning of its dangers.

13 Herman E. Daly, 'From Adjustment to Sustainable Development: The Obstacle of Free Trade' in *The Case Against Free Trade*, ibid., pp. 126-7.

14 On Oakeshott and Santayana, see my book, *Post-liberalism: studies in political thought*, London and New York: Routledge, 1992, Chapters 2 and 6.

15 That the disposition to constitute for themselves particular local identities is universal among human beings was maintained by J. G. Herder and other thinkers of what Isaiah Berlin terms the Counter-Enlightenment. For an exposition and assessment of such views in the context of an exploration of Berlin's contemporary attempt to reconcile them with liberalism, see my book *Berlin*, Harper/Collins (Fontana Modern Master), London, November 1994.

16 M. Oakeshott, *Rationalism in Politics and other Essays*, Indianapolis: Liberty Press, 1991, p. 410.

17 On this remarkable case, see my *Post-liberalism*, op. cit.

18 Edward Goldsmith, *The Way: an ecological world-view*, London: Rider, 1992, Chapter Eight.

19 George Santayana, *Dominations and Powers: Reflections on Liberty, Society and Government*, New York: Charles Scribner and Sons, 1951, p.340.

20 On Mill's idea of the stationary state, see my book, *Beyond the New Right: markets, government and the common environment*, London and New York: Routledge, 1994, Chapter 4, 'An Agenda for Green Conservatism'.

21 For an exception, see Fred Ikle, *National Review*, February 1994.

22 I owe my understanding of the embeddedness of economic institutions in cultural traditions to conversations with Edward Goldsmith.

23 See my *Beyond the New Right*, op. cit., Chapter Three, 'The Moral Foundations of Market Institutions'.

24 I refer to the liberal political philosophy of Joseph Raz, which I have discussed in my *Beyond the New Right*, ibid.

25 I have discussed the untransparency of value, and its implications for liberal theory, in my book, *Post-liberalism*, op. cit., Chapter 20, 'What is dead and what is living in liberalism'.

26 For a statement of this criticism of Raz, see B. Parekh, 'What's wrong with liberalism', *Times Literary Supplement*, February 25, 1994.

27 For a statement of this communitarian view, see Michael Sandel, *Liberalism and the Limits of Justice*.

28 The best contemporary exposition of this reactionary view is probably Roger Scruton's *The Meaning of Conservatism*.

29 David Willetts, *Civic Conservatism*, Social Market Foundation, June 1994.

30 I have discussed the idea of a negative capital tax in my *Beyond the New Right*, p. 153 ; and I have criticised Neo-Liberal proposals for a negative income tax in Chapters 1 and 3 of the same book.

31 David Ricardo, *Principles of Political Economy and Taxation*, London : J.M. Dent and Co., 1911, pp.266-7. Ricardo's conclusions about the deleterious impact of machinery on the interests of labourers have been supported by Paul Samuelson in his 'Mathematical Vindication of Ricardo on Machinery' in *Journal of Political Economy*, 96 (1988), pp. 274-82, and 'Ricardo was Right!' in *Scandinavian Journal of Economics*, 91, 1989, pp. 47-62. An excellent critique of the conventional arguments for free trade is to be found in the papers collected in *The Case Against Free Trade: GATT, NAFTA, and the Globalization of Corporate Power*, San Francisco: Earth Island Press, 1993. I am indebted to Edward Goldsmith for drawing this invaluable book to my attention.

32 Sir James Goldsmith, op. cit.

33 I attempt such a *tour d'horizon* in Chapter 4 of my *Beyond the New Right*, 'An Agenda for Green Conservatism'. I hold still to most of the views on policy defended there, without wishing to defend them mainly in conservative terms.

34 See my *Beyond the New Right*, ibid., Chapter 3.

35 I have developed a case for voucher schemes for schools, drawing not on Neo-Liberal thought but on the work of Ivan Illich, in my 'Agenda for Green Conservatism', in my *Beyond the New Right*, Chapter 4.

PAPERS IN PRINT

REPORTS

OCCASIONAL PAPERS

1	*Deregulation* David Willetts	£3.00
2	*'There is no such thing as society'* Samuel Brittan	£3.00
3	*The Opportunities for Private Funding in the NHS* David Willetts	£3.00
4	*A Social Market for Training* Howard Davies	£3.00
5	*Beyond Unemployment* Robert Skidelsky, Liam Halligan	£6.00
6	*Brighter Schools* Michael Fallon	£6.00

OTHER PAPERS

Local Government and the Social Market George Jones	£3.00
Full Employment without Inflation James Meade	£6.00